JUL   2003

OCEANIA

Cultures and Costumes Series:

CULTURES AND COSTUMES: SYMBOLS OF THEIR PERIOD

OCEANIA

CHARLOTTE GREIG

MASON CREST PUBLISHERS

www.masoncrest.com

Mason Crest Publishers Inc.
370 Reed Road
Broomall, PA 19008
(866) MCP-BOOK (toll free)
www.masoncrest.com

First printing 2002

1 2 3 4 5 6 7 8 9 10

Library of Congress Cataloging-in-Publication Data available

ISBN 1-59084-432-7

Printed and bound in Malaysia

Editorial and design by
Amber Books Ltd.
Bradley's Close
74–77 White Lion Street
London N1 9PF

Project Editor: Marie-Claire Muir
Designer: Hawes Design
Picture Research: Lisa Wren

Picture Credits:
All pictures courtesy of Amber Books Ltd, except the following:
The National Library of Australia: 8, 22-23, 26–27, 32, 35, 36, 39.

ACKNOWLEDGMENT
For authenticating this book, the Publishers would like to thank
Robert L. Humphrey, Jr., Professor Emeritus of Anthropology,
George Washington University, Washington, D.C.

Contents

Hawaii

Philippines

Malaysia

Indonesia

Papua New Guinea

Vanuatu

Fiji

New Caledonia

Australia

New Zealand

Oceania refers to the great expanse of sea, land, and islands that lie between Asia and America. To the west, this includes parts of Malaysia and Indonesia, while to the east, it covers Australia, New Zealand, Papua New Guinea, and the small islands of the South Pacific.

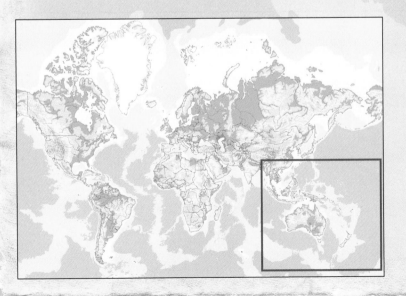

Introduction

Nearly every species in the animal kingdom adapts to changes in the environment. To cope with cold weather, the cat adapts by growing a longer coat of fur, the bear hibernates, and birds migrate to a different climatic zone. Only humans use costume and culture—what they have learned through many generations—to adapt to the environment.

The first humans developed their culture by using spears to hunt the bear, knives and scrapers to skin it, and needles and sinew to turn the hide into a warm coat to insulate their hairless bodies. As time went on, the clothes humans wore became an indicator of cultural and individual differences. Some were clearly developed to be more comfortable in the environment, others were designed for decorative, economic, political, and religious reasons.

Ritual costumes can tell us about the deities, ancestors, and civil and military ranking in a society, while other clothing styles can identify local or national identity. Social class, gender, age, economic status, climate, profession, and political persuasion are also reflected in clothing. Anthropologists have even tied changes in the hemline length of women's dresses to periods of cultural stress or relative calm.

In 13 beautifully illustrated volumes, the *Cultures and Costumes: Symbols of their Period* series explores the remarkable variety of costumes found around the world and through different eras. Each book shows how different societies have clothed themselves, revealing a wealth of diverse and sometimes mystifying explanations. Costume can be used as a social indicator by scientists, artists, cinematographers, historians, and designers—and also provide students with a better understanding of their own and other cultures.

ROBERT L. HUMPHREY, JR., Professor Emeritus of Anthropology,
George Washington University, Washington, D.C.

Papua New Guinea

Oceania has a stunning array of exotic costumes, ranging from the tribal headdresses and body adornment of the South Sea Islanders, to the ancient batik and *ikat* designs of Malaysia and Indonesia.

The term "Oceania," in its broadest sense, refers to the great expanse of sea, land, and islands that lies between Asia and America. To the west, this includes parts of Malaysia and Indonesia, while to the east, it covers Australia, New Zealand, Papua New Guinea, and the small islands of the South Pacific. Theories about how the native populations arrived in the islands vary. Some scholars have argued that people migrated there from America and Europe, but most now agree that Southeast Asians were the first to settle the region.

The largest island in Oceania, and the second largest in the world, is Papua New Guinea—directly north of Australia. Today, the island is divided into two parts: the western part is self-governed, and the eastern part, Irian Jaya, belongs to Indonesia. This division is the outcome of the island's complex and often

This Bena Bena Highlander from Papua New Guinea is wearing a headdress of cassowary feathers and a headband of green scarab beetles. His necklace is made of large white shells.

turbulent history. Since the 19th century, the Dutch, the Germans, the British, the Australians, and the Indonesians have all colonized it.

Papua New Guinea has an extraordinary variety of landscape and climate, ranging from dense tropical forests to rugged mountain ranges, and boasts a wealth of animal and plant life. However, for many, the most fascinating feature of the island is its tribal people. There are numerous native tribes on the island, in both the eastern and western parts, speaking more than 700 languages. Despite years of colonization, many of these tribes continue a Stone Age way of life that has survived unchanged for thousands of years. This is particularly true of the Highland tribes, which live in the remotest regions of the island. Until the 1930s, when gold miners brought back news of human habitation in the Highlands, Europeans did not even know of the tribes' existence there.

Many **anthropologists** and other scholars are eager to learn from such an early intact civilization. Yet, because many of the tribes' customs are secret, such as their initiation ceremonies for boys attaining adulthood, there is still much to learn about the true meanings of their ancient rites.

Sing-Sings

Today, many tourists visit the islands to see the tribes at sing-sings, events where native people dress up, dance, and chant. These sing-sings are not actually traditional rituals. The colonial government introduced them after World War II as a way of promoting peace between the tribes, which were often in conflict at the time. However, the events are still an ideal way to present the traditional dances, songs, and dress of the Papuans. The appearance of the tribe members is especially stunning, with an impressive array of adornment, from exotic plumed headdresses and **macabre** masks to brightly colored face paint, and designs plastered onto the body using mud.

This Papuan warrior wears a saber called a *peda* around his neck, along with an amulet in the shape of a human figure. His hair is decorated with a plume of feathers and a wooden comb.

Most of the island's tribes follow a social pattern of segregating men and women. The men live together and meet at spirit houses, conducting ceremonies in secret. The women usually live in separate groups from the men, tending to children and animals. The most prized animal on the island is the pig; pigs often live in houses with human families.

The *Bilum*

For their everyday chores, the women carry a *bilum*, a flexible string bag made of woven fiber, which they knot on their head and carry on their back. The *bilum* has a variety of uses, from carrying babies to transporting food. In addition to being a useful object, the *bilum* is also thought to have sacred properties that symbolize the role of the woman; for example, it may be used to collect and cradle a relative's bones after death. Today, many tribal women on the island sell *bilums* to

the tourists, but these are often made, not of plant fiber, but of brightly colored nylon string from Hong Kong.

Men also wear the *bilum*, decorated with feathers from the turkey, the **hornbill**, and other birds. The rarest, most prized feathers are those of the **cassowary**, which is difficult to catch and must be hunted by a man wearing a tiny "seed *bilum*," a bag woven around a seed that is thought to give him magical powers. Groups of men decorate the *bilums* in secret, as part of a boy's initiation into manhood. Along with the *bilum*, the boy is given objects, such as face paint and pig fat to grease his body. Then a secret ritual takes place to mark his passage into the adult world of men.

Spirit Masks

The tribes of Papua New Guinea are deeply religious, with a complex belief system of **totems** and **taboos**. Most of them have a place, animal, or natural object that they worship, such as a mountain, a monkey, or the sun. For example, the Iatmul tribe of the Sepik River region worships a giant crocodile. Along with their totems, or gods, the tribes also have a system of prohibitions, called *tapu* (related to the English word *taboo*). For example, menstruating women are

White shells decorate this Papuan tribesman's shield and hat. His hat is made of leaves, and his woolen tunic has a fringed hem. His shoulder belt is decorated with feathers.

In the Admiralty Islands, tribesmen paint their faces white and decorate their hair with hibiscus flowers and feathers. This warrior wears a white ring of shells as a chest ornament.

thought to be dangerous and, therefore, they must stay away from men during their periods. By observing the *tapu*, the tribes hope to be protected from evil spirits.

The Papuan tribes make many masks for a variety of religious purposes: to please their gods, to ensure good harvests, to protect tribes from sickness, to call down their ancestors, and so on. The most impressive of these are gigantic spirit masks made of feathers or from *tapa*, a cloth made from tree bark, mounted on huge **rattan** frames worn by the dancers. The dancers parade through the villages, singing and chanting. After the ceremony, the feather masks are dismantled and the feathers kept; the *tapa* masks are burned.

There are many other types of masks representing sacred spirits. For example, there are double-headed masks, masks with dangling tongues, masks with big, misshapen lips, and masks with huge coils of plant fiber and human hair wrapped about the face. One of the most striking of these is the hook-nosed "water spirit" mask, found on the islands around the coast of Papua New Guinea and in New Caledonia. Not all these masks are made to be worn. Some are worshiped as idols and thought to

This Papuan is dressed in a traditional grass skirt. His hair is whitened with a powder made from ground coral and then decorated with shells and feathers, including a yellow plume from a bird of paradise.

have supernatural powers to bring good or evil to the tribe (if they rot, for example, this can be a warning sign that something bad will happen); others may be attached to canoes or kept in the spirit houses to bring good luck.

To Westerners, these masks can look disturbing, ugly, and bizarre. This is because, in some cases, the masks are actually designed to look frightening so that they will ward off evil spirits. In other cases, they represent an ideal of beauty and a spiritual belief system that are different from our own.

Clothing

In general, the tribes of Papua New Guinea wear little clothing, although as they have more contact with Westerners, this tradition is changing. Both men and women traditionally wear grass skirts made of **raffia** and other vegetable fibers. These are worn short or long, and may be tiered, or layered, with colored strands. The men also wear loincloths. In some regions, such as the Oro Province, such clothes as capes and skirts are made from *tapa* and decorated with patterns of diagonal lines and dots; however, these are usually worn for special occasions instead of for everyday wear. Some tribes, such as the Dani, wear no clothing at all, except grass skirts for the women and penis sheaths for the men. The Yali, who were not in contact with white people until missionaries visited them in the 1960s, also wear nothing but rattan waist hoops and penis gourds. These sheaths are made from the dried shells of squashes and are sometimes held on by a string around the waist.

Body Adornment

Although few clothes are worn, the island tribes have complex ways of adorning their bodies, wearing an elaborate array of headdresses, jewelry, piercings, and face and body paint, all representing the beliefs and way of life of their tribe. For example, the Huli wear headpieces made from their own hair. At the age of 16, Huli boys enter a segregated village. They are allowed no contact with women for 18 months, during which time they grow their hair. The hair is then cut and made into "wigman" headdresses, which are decorated with flowers and feathers. These are worn for ceremonial occasions with hornbill necklaces and other adornments. The Huli are one of the most traditional tribes on the island, and still stage battles with enemy tribes, although these are now carefully planned and controlled.

Another tribal people who adorn themselves in a striking fashion are the Mudmen of Asaro. For ceremonies and sing-sings, they cake their bodies in dried mud, which gives them a strange, ghostly appearance. Legend has it that during one of their tribal wars, the Mudmen were driven into a river and became covered in mud. Later, as they made their way home, the mud dried. They then came across an enemy tribe, which ran away, frightened by their appearance. Mud and body paint are also used to represent animals. Some sing-sing dancers, for instance, wear long bamboo sticks on their fingers and paint their bodies in a stripe pattern to look like zebras.

A Changing Culture

Since the 19th century, many changes in tribal culture came about as the island's inhabitants began to grow cash crops and work for wages, for example, as miners. In addition, Christian missionaries have made a big impact on the culture, and many tribes have converted to Christianity. Certain practices, such as cannibalism (the eating of human flesh) and headhunting, in which the heads of slain enemies are cut off and displayed as trophies, have now been eradicated on the island, except perhaps in some remote inland areas.

Bilas

Many types of traditional jewelry, called *bilas*, are worn for dances. Necklaces, bracelets, headbands, armbands, and legbands are made of fibers and many kinds of shells. The islanders value shells highly, especially the gold-lipped pearl shell called *kina*, which is cut into crescent shapes. There are also shells called *toeia*, which are cut into disc shapes and used as necklaces and nosepieces. Modern currency on the island is named after these shells, and in some remote areas, the shells are still used as money.

All types of teeth are used to make jewelry—for example, crocodile, bat, porpoise, and dog teeth. Pig tusks are also worn as necklaces and nosepieces to show wealth. Some tribes wear human bones of dead relatives or enemies to attract spiritual power.

These social changes are reflected in the island people's dress; for example, among some Christian tribes, women now wear the feathered *bilums* that traditionally belonged to men only. Today, many native tribespeople, both men and women, have adopted Western items of dress, such as t-shirts and shorts. However, as modernization fails to bring wealth to the vast majority of the islanders, many of them have revived their ancient arts of mask- and headdress-making and body adornment. The expanding tourist trade, while it has brought some problems to the island, has also, to some degree, encouraged the revival of tribal traditions among the people of Papua New Guinea. In particular, the sing-sing events organized all over the island, where tribes gather to dance, sing, and show off their costumes, provide a glorious spectacle of costume and body art. From vibrant plumed headdresses and beautiful white-shell jewelry, to grotesque, frightening masks and ghostly mud-covered bodies, the culture and costumes of Papua New Guinea are a fascinating reminder of the sheer intensity, range, and power of the human imagination.

A warrior from the New Hebrides wears a hook-nosed wooden mask. His chest decoration is made of braided bullrushes and teeth pendants. His spear has barbs made from human bones.

The Islands of the South Pacific

The islands around Papua New Guinea are grouped together under the name Melanesia. They are home to some of the most exotic costumes and body adornment practices, including tattoo, in the world.

In ancient times, "Melanesia" meant "islands of the dark-skinned people," referring to the seafarers, probably from Southeast Asia, who first sailed there thousands of years ago. The way that these seafarers voyaged across a huge expanse of ocean in canoes to settle on tiny, windswept coral islands has astounded many scholars. Clearly, the "dark-skinned people" must have developed highly sophisticated systems of navigation to guide them through the seas in their small vessels. Today, there is evidence that their knowledge of the sea passages among the islands was passed down in the form of secret songs and chants, and that they wrote charts and maps using sticks and cowrie shells.

The Melanesians had a strong belief in magic; canoe captains, for example, cast spells to stop storms at sea. Yet they also had a rational understanding of

This man comes from Nukahiwa in the Marquesas group of islands. The warriors of the Marquesas were the most heavily tattooed people in Polynesia. Their tattoos were designed to frighten enemies in battle.

navigation, using the stars, cloud formations, bird migration patterns, and wind direction to calculate their position and to predict the weather as they sailed through the Pacific.

The islands around Papua New Guinea have strong cultural links with each other, dating back to these early times. However, each group of islands has developed its own distinctive way of life, emphasizing different aspects of the culture of the South Pacific.

The *Dukduk*

Lying off the coast of Papua New Guinea, New Britain is home to the Tolai people, in addition to other tribes. The Tolai had two male secret societies, the Iniet and the Dukduk. The Iniet held ceremonies to initiate young men into the society, wearing painted masks made of human skull bones decorated with hair. The Dukduk society had a terrifying ritual representing violent spirits who judged human beings and dealt out punishment for wrongdoing. There were two types of costume: the *dukduk* for the men and the *tubuan* for the women. Both of these were large, cone-shaped costumes, with a skirt of leaves around the bottom. The *dukduk* costume was faceless, while the *tubuan* had round eyes and a crescent-shaped mouth.

It was believed that the *dukduk* spirit lived at the bottom of the sea and could only be summoned onto land by the old men of the tribe. The old men of the tribe conspired together in secret to stage the ceremony, which could not be witnessed by women. The *dukduk* ceremony traditionally took place on the day before a new moon. The young men would gather on the beach, and the canoes would appear from the water, with the *dukduk* spirits dancing on them; then the spirits would run around, frightening the tribe members until nightfall. The *dukduk* would then make their way to a small house in the bush to eat a meal specially prepared for them. Having eaten, they would come out and perform a male initiation ceremony, beating the young men of the tribe with bundles of cane. After they left, the *dukduk* house would be burned. In this way, the old men of the tribe ensured that they held power and were looked after and respected.

The *tubuan* was the female spirit who gave birth to the *dukduk*. The *tubuan's* role was to enforce the law and collect fines from those who had broken the tribe's rules. The fines were paid with shell money. If any culprits failed to pay the fine, their houses would be burned to the ground.

The sinister costumes of the *dukduk* and the *tubuan* were so effective that the old men managed to continue their reign of terror over the tribe for many years.

Body Adornment: The Solomon Islands

In the past, the inhabitants of the Solomon Islands had a reputation for being fierce. For example, when they killed an enemy, they would remove the head from the body and keep it, preserving it in some way. The

Warriors in the Solomon Islands often pierced their noses and hung ornaments from them. This warrior's hair is tied up with a bamboo comb and decorated with red fringes.

Melanesians believed that the soul of a person lived in the head, so that if they kept their dead enemy's head, they could inherit his soul. The head was sometimes mummified and then worn as a mask in ceremonies to bring power to the tribe and increase the fertility of crops, animals, and human beings.

On a less gruesome note, the Solomon Islanders were also known for their beautiful artworks, including jewelry inlaid with mother-of-pearl. The

This 19th-century wood engraving shows a missionary, Bishop Patterson, and his party hunted by Melanesian tribesman. Tales of tribal headhunting and cannibalism terrified missionaries, as well as explorers and traders in the South Seas.

islanders made *kapkaps*, round shell ornaments that were worn on the forehead and the breast. These featured designs of birds and animals, using clam, cowrie, and other shells, often inlaid with turtleshell and mother-of-pearl. The jewelers often chose the frigate bird as a subject, mainly because these birds were important to the tribes in showing, by their diving habits, where schools of bonito (tuna) lay in the sea.

Today, the Kwaio tribe of the Solomon Islands still makes jewelry using an ancient method of grinding the shell on a stone, then cutting out the design with a flint and staining it with dye from tree berries. Unlike many tribes in the South Pacific, the Kwaio have never converted to Christianity and stay away from outsiders, only coming down from their home in the island's mountains to the coast to sell their goods in the market. In addition to *kapkaps*, the islanders' traditional jewelry includes ornamental hair combs made of palm wood, using a style of wickerwork called *boré*, and necklaces made of shell discs and teeth, such as porpoise, pig, dog, and fruit bat. Tiny porpoise teeth were considered highly desirable, and tribes would often band together to fish for porpoises. The teeth were worn on necklaces, armbands, and earplug discs;

some of these were taken off when it was necessary to make a payment, and then the jewelry would be restrung.

Grass Skirts and Garlands: Micronesia

Apart from Melanesia, there are two other groups of islands in the South Pacific: Micronesia and Polynesia. The islands of Micronesia, which include Yap, Guam, and the Caroline Islands, have been inhabited for thousands of years. It is thought that at one time the island of Yap had a large empire, which was governed by the people's belief in sorcery instead of by economic or political domination. Their particular skill, the people believed, was to cause storms at sea.

Micronesian culture centers on music, dancing, and body adornment with tattoos. In the past, dances were performed on a platform made of canoes, and the dancers wore headdresses that looked like canoes.

This warrior's necklaces are made from the jaws of rats and bats, as well as pigs' teeth. His hair is teased out and decorated with a comb of parrot feathers.

For dancing ceremonies, the Yapese wore grass skirts and adorned themselves in leaves and garlands. Their headdresses were made of colored woven fibers and long, exotic, brightly colored feathers. For everyday wear, the women wore the *lavalava*, a wraparound skirt made of banana and hibiscus fibers, woven in geometric patterns of contrasting colors.

Unlike most islanders of the South Pacific, the Micronesians wove their textiles on looms. It is now thought that they brought their looms with them when they first migrated to the islands from Southeast Asia thousands of years ago. Some islands in Micronesia, such as Kosrae and Ponape, have since become famous for their weaving, in particular, for their beautiful sashes, which were traditionally worn by noblemen. These long sashes are intricately patterned and are sometimes made of imported wool and cotton, as well as banana fiber. They also feature tiny shells and imported colored beads.

In Kiribati, formerly the Gilbert Islands, a unique type of armor was once made using strong coconut fiber. A whole suit of armor included leggings, sleeves, and a helmet, as well as the main **tunic**. At the front of the tunic was a breastplate of tough sharkskin, and the helmet was sometimes covered with the spiny skin of a blowfish.

In addition to weaving, the Micronesians painted and decorated their houses, utensils, and canoes. However, most of their creative skill went into short-term activities, such as making garlands of flowers and costumes, adorning the body, singing, dancing, and storytelling. The idealized picture of the South Pacific as a land of permanent leisure, with dancing girls wearing grass skirts and garlands of flowers, perhaps has its basis in the gentle, relaxed way of life of the Micronesians.

By the 20th century, with the increasing influence of Western culture, most of the Micronesian islands had converted to Christianity and the ancient religions of the region were no longer practiced. In particular, the art of tattooing began to die out.

This is a piece of bark cloth, or *tapa,* brought back by a sailor on the HMS *Resolution,* in 1772. In Hawaii, bark cloth is called *kapa,* while in Tonga it is known as *ngatu.*

Tapa Cloth

Apart from Melanesia and Micronesia, the other group of islands in the South Pacific is Polynesia. These islands include—among many others—Fiji, Tonga, Tahiti, the Marquesas, Western and American Samoa, and, some 2,000 miles (3,200 km) to the north, Hawaii. The cultures of these islands vary a great deal, but in terms of dress, most of the islanders for many years relied on *tapa,* a material made of tree bark, for their clothes. Today, imported cotton cloth has replaced *tapa* on most of the islands, but in Tonga and Samoa, bark cloth is still made for use at home and for export abroad.

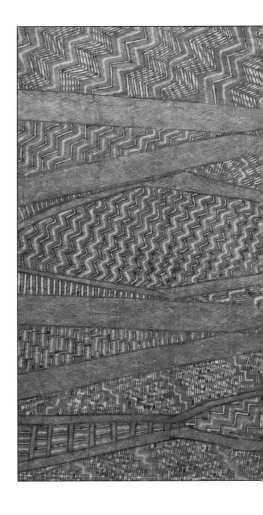

Traditionally, women make *tapa.* The cloth is made from the bark of the mulberry tree, which is the best kind, or from breadfruit and fig trees. Small trees are cut down and the bark peeled off in long strips. Then the outer bark is scraped off, leaving the white fiber inside. After the fiber is dried, it is soaked to soften it up. Then it is laid out over logs and beaten flat with a wooden beater, until the strips flatten out and join together. Eventually, a fine white cloth is made, which is then dyed or painted. In some parts of Polynesia, the plain white cloth is highly prized, but today, most *tapa* is decorated with designs that vary from island to island.

Tapa is usually painted or dyed in shades of brown, black, and red, although in the past, bright colors, such as purple, green, and blue, were used. For ceremonial use, dancers often paint their faces in the same kind of designs as

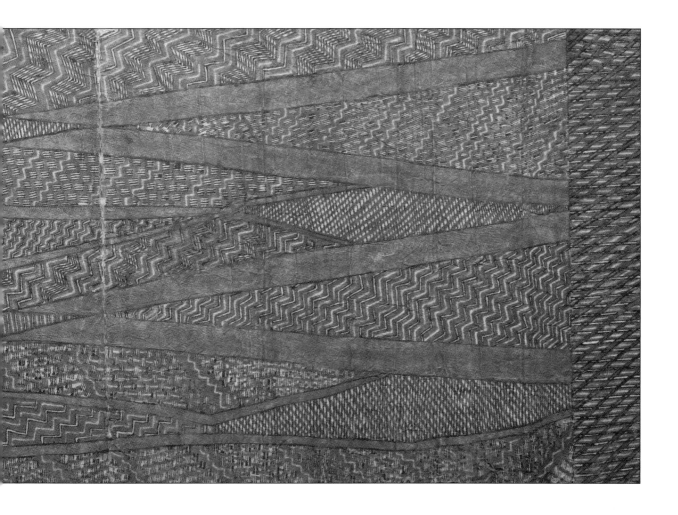

the *tapa* cloth, with dots and stripes in the same colors. *Tapa* is also used for making huge masks in and around Papua New Guinea. The Polynesians do not use masks as much as the Melanesians and Micronesians do, preferring to paint and tattoo their faces.

Tattoos

The word *tattoo*—or *tatu* in its native context—was first introduced into our language by English navigator and explorer Captain James Cook, who reported its use when he went to Tahiti in 1769. Since then, Europeans and Americans have been fascinated by the practice, which involves breaking the skin and introducing permanent dyes to form a pattern or design. Today, tattooing has become popular in the West. In some subcultures—for example, urban gangs—

Tattooed Warriors

The most striking tattoos in Polynesia were to be seen in the Marquesas Islands, where men were tattooed from head to foot with hundreds of complex, intricate designs. A favorite motif in the Marquesan designs was the turtle, accentuating the idea that the tattoo is a kind of protective "shell" for the wearer. In the Marquesas, which were inhabited by an unstable, warring society for much of its history, many of the men were warriors, and the tattoo functioned as a type of visual shield, dismaying and confusing the enemy. It also brought a man strength and special powers; for example, if many faces with eyes were tattooed on the body, the warrior would be able to see more clearly. Other Polynesian societies practiced different types of tattooing. In Samoa and Tonga, distinctive arched tattoos were made on the buttocks, hips, and thighs. In Fiji, the women, not the men, were tattooed in this way. In Tahiti, both men and women wore a variety of star and circle designs on the chest and arms, as well as arched tattoos on the buttocks and thighs.

the practice echoes the days when tribes marked their bodies to show their position in a clan or group by undergoing a painful and sometimes dangerous process. Ironically, in Polynesia, there are few native tribes that still practice the art; missionaries converted many of the tribes to Christianity and prohibited this and other native customs.

Although many anthropologists have studied Polynesian tattooing, the significance of it within the culture is not always clear. Undoubtedly, the designs were thought to be beautiful and of value as body adornment. But from island to island, the meaning of the tattoo varies. In some social systems, for example, tattoos are seen as a mark of rank or sexual **prowess**, while in others, this is not the case. What seems clear is that the painful process of tattooing was a type of initiation ritual, thought to strengthen the body and provide it with an "additional skin" or symbolic armor, permanently protecting it from harm. In some parts of the South Pacific, the more tender the body area—such as the eyelids, lips, and genitals—the more valuable the tattoos in these areas were thought to be.

Tatu was practiced throughout the whole of the South Pacific, in Micronesia and Melanesia, as well as Polynesia. The method usually involved dipping a small comb-like instrument, made of bone with a wooden handle, into a natural pigment or dye. The instrument was hammered into the skin again and again, creating a line of holes. These wounds were then left to heal, and the dye would permanently mark the skin. The process of tattooing could take hours, sometimes days, and in certain cases—for example, with Marquesan men—would continue at various stages throughout life.

Today, tattooing is still common among Samoans who have migrated to New Zealand and the United States. For those who have lost their traditional way of life in their homeland, it provides a link with the core values of their culture. For example, a popular tattoo design is that of the flying fox (a type of tropical bat), who is thought to protect her young beneath her wings. For Samoans, this design symbolizes care for a large extended family.

Feather Clothing for Royalty

Rank and position were more important in Tahiti and Hawaii than elsewhere in Polynesia. In the Society Islands (including Tahiti), ordinary people wore ponchos made of *tapa* (tree bark cloth) painted and printed with a variety of designs. For battle, high-ranking men wore long tubular headdresses decorated with feathers, teeth, and hair. For mourning, masks and aprons of mother-of-pearl were worn, along with feather cloaks. For everyday wear, tribe members carried fly whisks, often decorated with a carved figure on the end of the handle. Feather capes and elaborate fly whisks were associated with wealth and importance, but only chiefs were allowed to wear special decorative feather sashes called *maro* (the same name as was used for the ordinary male loincloth).

As each new ruler took his position, a new section of the sash would be added for him. The new feathers, usually red, would be sewn onto the flax base, using a needle made from a human bone and often involving human sacrifice. The feathers were believed to bring fertility. After the chief had worn the sash for his initiation, it was stored away until the next state occasion. It was believed that anyone who tried to steal the *maro* could be afflicted with disease so that he would go blind.

Headdresses and Jewelry

The men of Polynesia wore several types of flamboyant headdresses. One of these was a crown of white-shell strips and engraved tortoiseshell; another was a headband of mother-of-pearl with a tortoiseshell plaque above, carved and cut into a variety of designs. For jewelry, the Polynesians wore **pendants** made of whale teeth and other teeth, and reel-shaped necklaces. In Tonga, the islanders carved tiny female-shaped figures out of ivory and strung them together on necklaces. Later, when whaling made ivory more available as a material, the necklace figures became larger.

In Hawaii, feathers also had a sacred meaning and were closely identified with rank and position. Aristocratic men wore beautiful feather cloaks, capes, and helmets, especially in battle. The cloaks were made of red and yellow feathers that were gathered from small honeyeater birds. The feathers were attached to a strong netting of fiber. It took many hours of labor to hunt, collect, and sew the feathers for a large cloak, which might contain about half a million feathers taken from over 80,000 birds. Only in a society such as that of Hawaii, where rulers exploited their subjects mercilessly, could such labor-intensive royal clothing be made.

In addition to the royal cloak, the chief would carry a *kahili*, a feathered scepter, which was the sacred symbol of royalty. The *kahili* was often made of blue-black feathers from the frigate bird and bordered with red and yellow feathers above and below. Noblewomen wore feather *leis*, or garlands, around their necks and heads.

Today, there are many examples of Hawaiian featherwork cloaks and capes in museums all over the world, but few are made today. For the Hawaiians, the cloaks are perhaps too closely associated with the **autocratic** rulers of the past.

This warrior is a king's guard from the islands of Hawaii. He wears a yellow, red, and blue feather cloak and headdress to show his high status.

31

Australia and New Zealand

The native people of Australia, the Aborigines, have lived there for many thousands of years, while the Maori have lived on the islands of New Zealand for little more than a 1,000 years. Their societies developed in different ways, although each is relatively simple.

The Aborigines are the native peoples of Australia and Tasmania. They are thought to have lived there for thousands of years, establishing a **nomadic** way of life as **hunter-gatherers**, moving around the country in search of wild foods. Because the tribes were always on the move, they did not make many objects; possessions were not valued as a sign of wealth among the tribespeople. Instead, they developed a complex knowledge of the vast areas of land around them, mapping the land in their heads and in rock paintings so that they could follow ancient paths from watering place to watering place. In the north of Australia, they camped in bark shelters or, during monsoon season, in caves and huts on stilts. In the desert, they slept outside, making windbreaks of branches. The

This late 19th-century portrait shows a Maori mother and child. The mother's chin is tattooed in the traditional style of her tribe, and her cloak is decorated with kiwi feathers.

Aborigines' practical skills and knowledge of the country made them good hunters and helped them to survive in all types of terrain; but their relationship with the land was also a deeply spiritual one.

The Aborigines believed in "the Dreaming" or "Dreamtime," a spiritual realm where time and place did not exist. They thought that the spirits of their ancestors lived at certain sacred places, waiting to be reborn. Only the old men of the tribe had full knowledge of the dreaming, and they would relate it to the rest of the tribe through chants, stories, and paintings. The dreaming told the tribes that they were responsible for the fertility of the plants and animals around them, and also that they had a duty to care for each other unselfishly.

The Aborigines wore few clothes. When Captain James Cook visited Australia in 1770, he left gifts of cloth on the beach for the natives, but they did not regard them as having value and left them there. Some of the

Early Aborigines wore few clothes, but they painted their bodies with white chalk. They did not use bows and arrows for hunting. Instead, their weapons included spears and boomerangs, which are curved wooden missiles that return to the thrower.

Corroborees

When Europeans arrived in Australia, there were between 300,000 and a million Aborigines living there. Today, Aborigines constitute only about two percent of the population. Since the 18th century, a combination of war, disease, and poverty has wiped out most of the tribes. In the process, much of their culture has been lost, but there is currently an attempt to revive it. Aboriginal history is told in *corroborees* (song and dance events), and aboriginal "dreamtime" designs are printed onto boomerangs and t-shirts for export. In the *corroborees*, some ancient customs survive. For example, the Aborigines believed that white is the color of the returning dead, so this is still used for body painting. In addition, red ocher face paint, shell or bone necklaces, and bone nose ornaments are still worn.

Aborigines' early rock paintings show figures—some with animal heads—wearing ornaments and carrying spears and boomerangs. Other pictures show ceremonial fans made of marsh-bird feathers. Among the **artifacts** that have been found in Australia are stone pendants, animal-teeth necklaces, and bone pins, suggesting that the early Aborigines wore animal-skin cloaks.

The Maori

The Maori tribes of New Zealand are Polynesian in origin, and they share many aspects of their culture with their neighbors in Tahiti and the other Polynesian islands. They fared better than the Aborigines under colonial rule, and more aspects of their culture remain intact, despite the ravages of war, disease, and poverty since the 18th century.

It is thought that the Maori originally traveled from other Polynesian islands to New Zealand in the ninth century A.D. Like the Aborigines, the Maori had a close relationship with the land. However, unlike the natives of Australia, they developed a structured society in which ownership of land and social status were important. Chiefs inherited their titles and ruled over the people, and marriages were conducted in recognition of the land ownership within the tribe. Although there was a strict social hierarchy among the Maori, there was also an acknowledgment that all tribe members shared a common ancestry.

The early Maori tribes wore little clothing. The women wore leaves around the waist and a cloak for warmth. They may also have worn bark-cloth skirts brought from the other Polynesian islands. For the men, there was a rule that the glans of the penis must be covered, so the penis foreskin was pulled over it by a string attached to a belt.

This Maori group is sitting by a canoe carved in traditional Maori style. The girls wear cloaks and skirts made from *taaniko*, a type of flax. The girl on the right wears a *tiki* pendant.

Faces of Courage

The Maori tattooed themselves heavily, especially on the face. Their tattoo designs for the face were similar to the curves and scrolls they used in wood carving. Men tattooed the whole of their faces, whereas the women's faces were tattooed only around the mouth and chin. Each person had an individual design; the tattoos represented their courage in undergoing the pain of the process. The *tatu* artist was highly regarded in the tribe and ranked as a priest with special knowledge of the sacred rituals of his art.

Maori men went into battle dressed only in a war belt made of flax, which held a club; in their hands, they carried a spear or sword. Their buttocks were heavily tattooed so that they would look impressive in battle. In peacetime, high-ranking Maori men often carried their weapons as part of their formal attire. Weapons were beautifully carved and ornamented to show a man's high status and the respect the tribe accorded to him. The **adze**, for example, had a carved handle and a long blade made of jade, a hard green stone that could only be carved by patiently rubbing it down with sandstone.

Weaving looms were unknown to the early Maori. They wove clothes in *taaniko*, a type of finger-weaving using flax. They dyed their clothes in red, black, and white colors. Maori women wore flax skirts with a red or black underskirt and headbands with or without feathers. They also wore large pendants called *tiki* made of jade. The *tiki* were passed down through families and were thought to increase their wearers' fertility. The women also wore ear adornments made of shark's teeth.

The men wore a kind of kilt or grass skirt known as a *piupu*, which was made of strands of flax. Both sexes wore cloaks made from a variety of materials, including kiwi and parrot feathers. In the 18th century, after Captain

The face of this Maori man is covered with the scroll pattern of a traditional Maori tattoo, yet he is wearing Western clothing. Feathers adorn his hair.

Cook's first visit to New Zealand, many types of bark cloth were imported from Tahiti. European missionaries also introduced new styles of clothing: to cover their breasts, the women now wore bodices, patterned in *taaniko*, while the men adopted shirts and bandoliers, a kind of broad, over-the-shoulder belt worn by European soldiers at the time.

Today, there has been a revival of Maori culture, including tattoos and costume. Most Maori people no longer tattoo their faces, but paint them in the traditional patterns of the tribes. Ceremonial cloaks are still worn for special occasions, such as weddings and funerals.

Malaysia, Singapore, and the Philippines

Malaysia consists of the southern half of the Malay Peninsula (except Singapore) and the parts of northwestern Borneo known as Sarawak and Sabah. Half the population is Malay; the other half is made up of Chinese (the second largest ethnic group) and Indians. This ethnic mixture has led to a stunning array of costumes and textiles.

The *baju melayu* is the traditional dress of Malay men. A sarong or pair of pants is worn with a loose shirt, sometimes a long sash or belt, and the outfit is completed with a small velvet hat, peaked at the sides and with a dent in the middle, called a *songkok*.

The traditional Malay costume for women is called the *baju kurung* and consists of a loose tunic worn over a long skirt. For funerals, a white *baju* is

Malaysia is home to peoples of many different cultures. On the far left is a Dayak woman; in the center is a tribal warrior; and to the right is a girl from the aristocracy.

The Sarong

The costume of Malaysia reflects the three main ethnic groups: Malay, Chinese, and Indian. For the Malays, the traditional dress is the sarong, a simple length of fabric that is wrapped around the lower body and tied at the waist. Above the sarong, women wear long-sleeved blouses and men wear shirts. Although this style of dress is essentially simple, the fabrics used to make the garments are quite stunning. Sarongs are made of fabric dyed and woven in a number of ways to make beautiful patterns.

In addition to fabric dyeing, weaving techniques are used to make sumptuous garments for weddings and other celebrations. Silks are woven in different colors to reflect the light, shot through or embroidered with silver and gold thread. Different regions are known for their unique materials and styles of dress. For example, Terengganu is famous for its cloth, while the Bajan people in Sabah wear jackets embroidered in gold and white.

worn as a mark of respect. The *kebaya* is a more revealing modern women's costume: a tight blouse is worn with a long sheath of **batik** as a skirt, pleated and tied around the waist. The *kebaya* is frowned on by many Muslims in Malaysia, who regard it as immodest. For Muslim women, the traditional Malay *selendang*, a long scarf that covers the head or is worn on the shoulder, is a practical way of meeting religious dress requirements.

The Chinese also have their own costumes. Long before silks were imported to the West, the Chinese had developed many ways of producing and weaving this luxurious fabric. Today, Chinese clothing in Malaysia reflects a mixture of Eastern fabric techniques and Western styles. The *cheongsam*, as it is called in Cantonese, is a close-fitting, side-fastening dress with a high Mandarin collar, often made of patterned or embroidered silk. The *samfu*, another Chinese costume, is a side-fastening jacket and matching trousers, often made of cotton.

The Indians of Malaysia also wear their national dress, according to their ethnic background and caste, or class. For formal occasions, the women wear a short bodice and a colorful sari, a long piece of cloth worn over the shoulder and wrapped around the waist, while the men wear a variety of clothing, including knee-length coats over wide trousers.

The Dayak

The Dayak are the **indigenous** people of Borneo, meaning that they are native to the island. Today, Borneo is divided into Malaysian Sarawak and Sabah and Indonesian Kalimantan; the Dayak people, who number about two million, live in both parts of the island, but the largest number are in Sarawak. *Dayak* is a general term used to describe all the indigenous people of the region, and it is often vaguely applied to different tribes. For example, in Sarawak there are so-called Land Dayak and Sea Dayak. The Sea Dayak are actually a tribe called the Iban.

This Dayak woman wears a cotton sleeveless jacket and sarong. On her back is a traditional baby carrier made of woven rattan. Babies of high status in the tribe have carriers decorated with coins and animal teeth.

Dayak men wearing hunting and battle dress. The loincloth (left) and breastplate (right) are made of vegetable fibers. The tribesmen's hairstyles show the influence of Polynesian dress.

The Iban people live in large communal houses by the side of rivers, like most of the Dayak tribes. There are no class distinctions among the Iban. In other tribes, such as the Kayan and the Kenyah, there are three levels of society: chiefs, common people, and a lower class of people. Most of the Dayak tribes grow rice as their staple, or main, food, and some hunt and fish as well. In the past, they were known as fierce warriors with a reputation for headhunting, that is, removing the heads of their victims and displaying them as trophies. Today, the Dayak live more peacefully, although there has been some unrest in recent years as they defend their territories and ancient way of life.

The Dayak still wear many items of traditional dress, including the Dayak baby carrier, a rattan basket on a wooden frame worn on the back and decorated with woven patterns and beaded embroidery. To protect the baby and bring him or her good luck, coins and animal teeth are sewn on in beautiful patterns. The Dayak are also known for their beautiful woven cloth, which they wear for ceremonial events, often with medallions attached to the fabric. The Iban also wear silver belts for ritual dances.

Singapore

Singapore is located at the southern end of the Malay Peninsula. The city of Singapore lies on an island of the same name, surrounded by 60 small islands that form the Republic of Singapore. It is connected to West Malaysia by a causeway. Its position at the tip of Malaysia means that it has always been an important port; today, it is a thriving, industrial city with a leading role in the economy of Southeast Asia. In the past, the British colonized it. In 1963, it became part of Malaysia; then it became an independent state two years later.

Like Malaysia, Singapore is a multiethnic society, made up of people from many different parts of the world. Malay, Chinese, Indian, and European cultures all play a part in its history. Its importance over the centuries as a center for trade—both within the countries of Asia and later with Europe—and its status today as a center of global commerce mean that its population is one of the most ethnically varied in the world.

Although there has been political conflict with Malaysia over the years, Singapore is culturally similar to its neighbor, except that the European element in its history is British instead of Dutch. Singaporeans like to project a modern image, but there is still an attachment to tradition. For example, advertisements for Singapore Airlines for many years showed air hostesses wearing the *baju kebaya*, the tightly fitting blouse and batik sarong.

Native Tribes of the Philippines

The 7,000 islands of the Philippines are home to over 100 ethnic groups. Today in the Philippines, as in Malaysia, many people wear Western dress. However, there are native peoples in the mountainous Central Cordillera region of Luzon who still lead a traditional way of life.

The Igorot, as they were named by the Spanish and those living on the coastal lowlands, are in fact many main tribes, including the Ibaloy, the Kankanay, the Ifugao, the Apayo, the Gaddang, and the Bontoc. Some live in the tropical forests at the foothills of the mountain range, but most live on the

This warrior from Singapore is in traditional battle dress and carrying a lance and a blowpipe, the national weapon. Over his shoulder, he wears a leopard skin, and his headdress is made of feathers.

higher ground. In past times, they were renowned as headhunters, but during Spanish and then American colonization, this custom died out. The tribes mostly live in villages and grow rice, except for the Ifugao, who live in farmhouses on their rice terraces, and the Gaddang, some of whom live in tree houses.

Traditionally, most of the tribes wore little clothing. The children usually went naked, the men wore loincloths, and the women wore short skirts made of bark or other cloth. The men's loincloth was a strip of fabric known as a *bahag* worn around the waist and drawn between the legs, with the ends hanging loosely at the front. In time, cotton came to replace bark cloth, and the tribes began to develop their own patterns for the *bahags* to distinguish between different clans.

In colder weather, both men and women wore brightly colored woven blankets to keep warm. They ornamented themselves with jewelry made of beads, gold, agate, mother-of-pearl, and brass. Some tribes tattooed themselves as well. The conquistadores, adventurers from Spain who came to conquer and

The Philippines is home to many ethnic groups, including Chinese (shown here), Indian, Spanish, and native peoples. Filipino national costume has evolved as a mixture of these styles of dress.

colonize native peoples, called the tattooed people of the Western Visayan islands *pintados*, meaning "painted people."

The men of the Igorot tribes usually carry spears with them as part of their traditional dress. Today, the tribespeople continue to use their skills in weaving and iron and brass metalwork; their blankets, headbands, ornamental spears, and jewelry are sold across the world to tourists and collectors.

Filipino National Dress

Over the centuries, cloth has been produced in the Philippines and used as a form of exchange. In northern Luzon, **indigo**-dyed cloth was prized and, in

This Filipino woman is wearing a *bara*, a type of short-sleeved blouse, and a *saya*, a type of skirt. Her hair is dressed in a traditional Filipino style.

Abra, blankets became a status symbol. Cloth was also woven from *abaca*, a native Filipino plant, a tradition that survived for many years in Mindanao. Another fabric was *piña*, made from the fibers of the pineapple plant. Raw silk from China was mixed with *piña* to make fabrics for export.

Since the 16th century, the traditional costumes of the Filipinos have been a mixture of indigenous, Spanish, Chinese, and Indian styles, reflecting the islands' history. For example, the *barong tagalog*, the official costume for Filipino men, is a combination of all these elements. It started life as the costume of the *indio* (native) laborers, being a light shirt called a *camisa* in Spanish, made of materials such as *piña* or cotton. Legend has it that the native peoples were made to wear these shirts to distinguish them from the colonials and to make sure they had no pockets to keep money in. Chinese tailors later added

Native Dance Costumes

The Igorot tribes have common religious beliefs, sacrificing animals to a number of spirit gods and performing dances to please their ancestors and bring good luck. In many of the dances, ceremonial clothes are worn. For example, the Bontoc perform a courtship dance in which each of the male and female dancers holds a square of brightly colored cloth, which is shaken to show sexual interest; in another dance, the young women show off their agility while carrying clay pots on their heads.

details such as embroidery and pleats to make a more formal shirt. In the 19th century, collar and cuffs were added in the Western style. Today, the *barong* is a long shirt with collar, cuffs, and side slits, worn outside the trousers.

Like the native men of the Philippines, the colonists required women to cover their upper bodies. They wore short-sleeved blouses called *baro* and wraparound skirts known as *saya*. The blouses were often made of thin, see-through fabrics, whereas the skirts were usually thicker. An overskirt or apron was added on top of the *saya*, and a square piece of cloth was worn on the head, also covering the upper part of the body. This is the costume that is now worn as female national dress in the Philippines.

Spanish and Chinese Styles

The meeting of Spanish, Chinese, and native styles in the Philippines has created some wonderful costumes through the centuries. At the end of the 19th century, the "Maria Clara" costume became fashionable, named after the *mestiza* (mixed Spanish and Filipino) heroine of a famous novel, *Noli Me Tangere*. It was a highly feminine outfit, consisting of a flimsy blouse with bell sleeves over a long, full *saya* skirt and tight overskirt. Over the low-cut blouse was worn a *panuelo*, an embroidered fabric to cover the bosom.

Over time, the *panuelo* and the overskirt were dropped as the *terno* came into fashion. The *terno* was a full skirt joined at the waist to a tightly fitting bodice, featuring butterfly sleeves and a low neckline. The bodice was often elaborately embroidered, and the skirt was folded, draped, and layered in many different ways, as fashion dictated.

Later, in the 1930s, another Filipino fashion developed: the *balintawak*. Like the Chinese *cheongsam* dress, this was a combination of Western and Eastern influences. The dress featured a low-cut bodice, a sash, and butterfly sleeves, and was worn for days out in the countryside. It symbolized relaxed yet sophisticated vacationwear for city dwellers from Manila who wanted to preserve a sense of their cultural roots, but be in time with Western fashion.

Indonesia

Indonesia is a republic made up of over 13,000 islands that lie off the coast of mainland Southeast Asia. Holland originally colonized the region, and it was known as the Dutch East Indies. It declared its independence after World War II. Like Malaysia, its mixture of Indian, European, and native peoples has led to rich and varied cultures and costumes.

The capital of Indonesia, Jakarta, is located on the island of Java. Indonesia consists of Java and Sumatra, the southern part of Borneo called Kalimantan, Sulawesi (formerly the Celebes), Bali, Sumba, Sava, Flores, Timor, the Moluccas (also known as the Spice Islands), and the western part of New Guinea known as Irian Jaya. There are many other smaller islands that also form part of Indonesia. Irian Jaya was recognized as part of Indonesia in 1969, and in the 1970s, Timor was incorporated. East Timor gained independence in 2002.

Indonesia is one of the most densely populated countries on earth. Its tropical climate and rich mineral deposits, along with a policy of intense foreign capital investment, make it one of the major agricultural and manufacturing economies of the world. Today, Indonesia is a land of contrasts: modern cities coexist with rural areas where time seems to have stood still. It is a place where traditional values, as well as a strong military presence, often seem to clash with the freedoms of a modern industrial society.

Java is known throughout the world for its beautifully woven textiles. The regent's sumptuous clothing and tall hat (left) show his high status.

Indonesia is a melting pot for people of many different cultures. Like Malaysia, it boasts a combination of indigenous people native to the islands, together with Chinese, Indian, and European populations. Because of its thriving economy since the 1960s, Indonesia has attracted workers from all over the world, who add their cultures, way of life, and costumes to what was already a rich, diverse, multiethnic society.

The Blouse and Sarong

In Indonesia's big cities, many people have adopted a Western style of dress. The men especially tend to wear Western suits and leisure clothes. However, among women, the *baju kebaya*, the traditional blouse and sarong, is still popular. As in Malaysia, the blouse is styled in different ways and the sarong is made of various fabrics, but certain elements remain the same. The blouses are made without **darts**, cut with inserts of fabric under the arms to ensure a good fit, while the sarong is a length of cloth pleated and tied at the waist with a cord called a *stagen*. In addition to the blouse and sarong, women often wear the *selendang*, a long scarf draped over one shoulder. This is especially important to Muslim women, whose religious beliefs require them to cover up their bodies.

Batik

For many years, the islands of Indonesia have been important centers of trade in exotic fabrics. In Java, a style of patterned fabric known as batik was developed; it became popular all over Southeast Asia and is now exported all over the world. Areas of the cloth are covered in melted wax so that they will not be colored when it is dyed. The wax is poured from a small kettle and then drawn into patterns with a pen-like wax holder called a *canting*. The uncolored parts of the cloth make a pattern, picture, or design, and the cloth is then boiled to remove the wax. After this, it is re-dyed so that the previously waxed sections come out in a contrasting color. Several colors can be used, dying

This man's shaven head shows that he is a Muslim. His traditional basin-shaped hat acts like a parasol, protecting his head and face from the sun.

different parts of the fabric not covered in wax. The traditional colors of batik are indigo and brown, but red and yellow have also been used for many years. The designs are often circles and diamond shapes; the finer fabrics include animal and plant forms with curved outlines.

It is not known when the batik method originated, but it has been practiced in Java for centuries. The traditional method of making the cloth is time-consuming; a single piece of fabric can take up to several weeks to complete. Today, the process has been speeded up with the introduction of copper stamps that mimic the effect of the old-fashioned, labor-intensive way of applying the wax.

Ikat

Another style of cloth that is popular in Indonesia is *ikat*, a complex form of tie dyeing. Before being woven, the threads of the cloth are made into bunches and then tightly tied at certain points. The bunches are then dyed, but the tied parts do not take any color. The process is repeated with various colors. When the thread is woven, the design takes shape, according to the different colors on the thread. Usually, only the warp (vertical) threads on the loom are dyed; the weft (horizontal) threads are left plain.

Dressed in the costume of the Minangkabau people of Sumatra, the girl on the right wears their unique women's headdress, a turban folded with two points in the shape of buffalo horns.

However, in Sumatra, the weft threads are dyed as well. This process produces a beautiful cloudy effect on the cloth. The patterns are normally simple, but in the finest *ikat* designs, there are complex representations of animals, birds, and other forms. In Bali, a process known as "double *ikat*" is practiced, and the resulting cloth is considered sacred. *Ikat* is technically difficult to make in the traditional way, and for centuries was a highly prized cloth that was seen as a sign of a family's wealth and status.

Buffalo Horns: The Minangkabau

In western Sumatra, the Minangkabau people are known for their unique culture and clothing. Their traditional houses have roofs with peaked ends in the shape of buffalo horns. Similarly, the Minangkabau women's traditional headdresses—turbans with sharp conical points—are folded to resemble buffalo horns. According to legend, the symbol of the buffalo came from a conflict between the Minangkabau and the Javanese, in which the two sides agreed to a buffalo fight to settle their differences. The Javanese buffalo was a strong animal, but the Minangkabau had only a little calf. Before the fight, the Minangkabau attached knives to the calf's horns and starved it of milk, so that when it saw the great buffalo it went to feed and pierced the buffalo's belly—the Minangkabau were victorious. Their name means "victory buffalo."

The Toraja of Sulawesi

Sulawesi, formerly known as Celebes, is another source of beautiful Indonesian textiles. The tribes on the island are known as Toraja, a general term covering all the native ethnic groups. The Sa'dan Toraja, one of these groups, are farmers and craftworkers renowned for their skill in making batik and *ikat* cloth. The houses they use for worshipping their ancestors are portable structures with boat-shaped roofs made of split bamboo. When a new house is made, the young women of the tribe perform a special dance wearing single-color sarongs and bodices to offset their decorative ceremonial costume of batik stoles, fringed overskirts, beaded collars, and headbands. In their belts, they carry sacred silver-hilted daggers called *kris*.

Following Balinese tradition, the married woman on the left has tied up her hair with flowers.

In addition to symbolizing the victory of the clever over the strong, the story illustrates the importance of the nurturing mother in Minangkabau culture. This is appropriate in a **matrilineal** culture in which names and property are passed down through the women instead of the men. Women play an important role in village councils and other aspects of community life. Today, many Minangkabau are Muslims, which clashes with their matrilineal heritage; however, compromises have been made to accommodate both ways of life.

There are a number of other tribes in Sumatra, such as the Mentawai and the Toba-Batak people. The traditional Mentawai dress is a simple loincloth; but for ceremonies and festivals, they wear beaded armbands decorated with flowers and flamboyant headdresses made of leaves, flowers, and raffia. The Toba-Batak are renowned for their beautiful cloth, which is handwoven, often in somber colors, like indigo and maroon. They use this cloth to make sarongs and *ulos*, long scarves or stoles worn over one shoulder. The men also wear flat hats with a red band around them.

Balinese Costume

In Bali, an independent culture has survived despite centuries of colonization. A mixture of Hinduism and ancient beliefs in the souls or spirits of natural objects characterizes Balinese religion. Balinese dress is also unique. Here, the *kebaya,* or top, is made of fine muslin or **organdie** with an *ikat* or batik sarong, sometimes decorated with silver and gold coins and threads. The bodice is often brightly colored with a floral design, while the sarongs are darker, often in blues and browns. A wide scarf is wrapped around the waist over the blouse. Alternatively, the women wear a matching bodice and sarong with a long scarf tied over the shoulder. In Bali, the unmarried women wear their hair in a braid to one side of the head; when they marry, they tie up their hair with flowers.

The islands of Sumbawa, Flores, and Timor are culturally linked to Bali— all belong to the Nusa Tengarra group of native people. There are different varieties of *ikat* on each island, and people wear sarongs and stoles in many different ways according to local traditions.

The Spice Islands

The Moluccas, a group of islands including Ambon, Banda, and Halmahera, were once known as the Spice Islands. Long before the arrival of the Portuguese in the 16th century, these islands exported cloves, nutmeg, and other spices all over Asia. The riches of the islands were the cause of much conflict over the centuries between the Portuguese, the Spanish, the English, and the Dutch. This history has resulted in a culture that is mixed, incorporating native, Malay, Polynesian, Indian, Chinese, and other influences.

On Banda, there are traces of colonialism in ceremonial native dances in which men wear red breeches and black jackets. They carry blunderbusses, an old-fashioned type of gun with a short musket used by the Dutch in the

19th century. In Halmahera, the native Giman people file down their teeth, a custom practiced since ancient times. In Babar, another Moluccan island, the men wear straw headbands and antique cloths known as *basta* for ceremonial dances. The cloths are thought to be Indian in origin and are worn folded over the chest and body to make a long apron at the front.

Java: Colors of Life

In Java, as in the whole of Indonesia, traditional clothing has a deep spiritual significance. Modern ways of life and influences from the West have changed many aspects of Javanese culture, but traditional codes of behavior and dress are still important—even though these may have been adapted over the years to accommodate different religious beliefs and social customs. In particular, there is a unique mix of Hindu and Islamic culture dating back to the 15th century.

Since ancient times, cloth has had a deep symbolic meaning for the Javanese. Whole villages band together to spin, weave, and dye cloth. Indigo dye is kept in large vats that are considered sacred. The wife of the village leader is the only person allowed to control the process of indigo dyeing, an art that she hands down to her daughter. For Javanese people, each color has a special

Grinsing

A special type of *ikat* cloth called *grinsing* is made in Bali. In accordance with the phases of the moon, certain plants are gathered to make dyes. The vertical and horizontal threads of the loom (the warp and the weft) are then tie-dyed to make a double-weave effect. The process is a complicated one, requiring a lot of skill, and a single piece of cloth can take up to nine years to make. The resulting piece of cloth is considered sacred, and, today, it is forbidden to export *grinsing* out of Indonesia.

This Javanese man and woman wear long full trousers gathered at the waist by a narrow belt. The woman wears two chains hanging from a gold, gem-studded collar, while the man wears a garland made of flowers.

significance. White is the color of rising sun in the east; yellow is the color of the west; red denotes the south, where the sun reaches its height; and black is where the sun sets at the end of the day. Corresponding to the sun's position in the sky are concepts of life, maturity, and death. Thus, children wear shoulder scarves of white; young girls wear red and white; older women wear patterned cloth on a yellow background; and widows wear a dark blue-and-brown cloth called *irengan*.

Today, Western dress is common in Java, especially among men. However, there is still a strong dress code determining the use of traditional cloth, whether for everyday wear or for special ceremonies. The type of cloth used in a sarong, bodice, stole, dress, or hat can tell the story of a person's life: what region or even village he or she comes from, what class he or she belongs to, his or her sex, and his or her age. Today, a great deal of cloth is made for export, and fashions from the West have become popular all over Indonesia. But the traditional cloth of these islands, and the many varied styles in which it is worn, continue to have a deep significance for Indonesians as part of their ancient spiritual heritage.

Glossary

Note: Specialist words relating to clothing are explained within the text, but those that appear more than once are listed below for easy reference.

Adze a cutting tool that has a thin arched blade set at right angles to the handle; used chiefly for shaping wood

Anthropologist a person who studies humanity around the world—its origins, societies, cultures, religious beliefs, and institutions

Artifact an object, such as a tool, piece of jewelry, or work of art, made by hand, usually following an ancient traditional method

Autocratic relating to a government in which one person posesses unlimited power

Batik an Indonesian method of hand-printing textiles by coating with wax the parts not to be dyed; a piece of fabric printed in this way

Cassowary a large flightless bird with shiny black feathers

Dart a stitched tapering fold in a garment

Hornbill a type of Asian or African bird with a large bill

Hunter-gatherer a member of an early tribe or social group that moved around the land hunting animals and gathering wild foods

Indigenous occuring naturally in a region or environment

Indigo a deep blue dye originally made from plants

Macabre dwelling on the gruesome

Matrilineal relating to or tracing descent through the maternal line

Nomadic relating to a people who have no permanent residence, but move from place to place, usually seasonally and within a well-defined territory

Pendant an ornament (such as one on a necklace) allowed to hang free

Prowess skill

Raffia the fiber of the raffia palm used especially for tying plants and making baskets and hats

Rattan a part of the stem of a rattan (a type of palm) used especially for walking sticks and wickerwork

Organdie a fine, transparent muslin with a stiff finish

Taboo a rule or system of rules forbidding certain activities according to spiritual beliefs or social custom

Totem a natural object, animal, place, or occurrence worshipped according to spiritual beliefs

Tunic a simple slip-on garment made with or without sleeves and knee-length or longer, belted at the waist, and worn as an outer or under garment

Timeline

SOUTH PACIFIC ISLANDS

2000 B.C.	The islands of Micronesia are first inhabited.
A.D. 1526	Papua New Guinea is discovered by Portuguese explorer Jorge de Meneses, who names it *Isla dos Papuas* (Island of the Fuzzy Hairs).
1772–1775	Captain James Cook finds more islands, including the Marquesas and Fiji.
1778	Cook discovers Hawaii, which he calls the Sandwich Islands, and is killed there the following year.
1789	HMS *Bounty* mutineers arrive in Tahiti.
1920	The Dutch hand Papua New Guinea over to Australia.
1963	Indonesia takes control of Dutch New Guinea, renaming it Irian Jaya.
1973	Papua New Guinea is granted self-government.

AUSTRALIA

38,000 B.C.	Aborigines first inhabit Australia.
A.D. 1432	The Chinese land at the future site of Darwin.
1616	The Dutch land in Australia.
1770	Captain Cook explores Australia.
1788	A British colony is established in New South Wales.
1842	Copper and gold deposits are discovered.
1901	The Commonwealth of Australia is proclaimed.

NEW ZEALAND

A.D. 800	Habitation of the region begins.
1624	The arrival of Dutch navigator Abel Tasman, the first European contact.
1769	Captain Cook encounters the Maori.
1840	The British assume control.
1907	New Zealand is declared independent.

MALAYSIA

2500 B.C.	Neolithic culture is established.
A.D. 1400	Sumatran exiles found the city-state of Malacca, which enters a golden age as a commercial Islamic center.
1511	The Portuguese capture Malacca.
1641	The Dutch take control of Malacca.
1600s	The Minangkabau people migrate from Sumatra to Malayasia.
1957	Malayasia achieves independence.

SINGAPORE

A.D. 1400s	Tumasik (Singapore) becomes part of the Malacca empire; the British establish the port of Singapore.
1959	Singapore becomes a self-governing state.
1963	Singapore is incorporated into Malaysia.
1965	Independence is declared.

THE PHILIPPINES

A.D. 1000	Chinese traders inhabit the islands.
1521	Ferdinand Magellan, the Portuguese explorer and navigator, discovers the islands.
1571	The Philippines become a Spanish colony.
1898	The Philippines are ceded to the United States.
1906	The Filipino independence movement is subdued.
1946	Independence is declared.

INDONESIA

1000 B.C. Migrations from mainland Asia are completed.

A.D.1200s Indian traders bring Islam to the region.

1511 The Portuguese arrive in the Moluccas; the Spanish, Dutch, and British later colonize Indonesia.

1945 Indonesia declares independence from the Netherlands.

1969 The United Nations recognizes Irian Barat as part of Indonesia.

1975–1976 The former Portuguese territory of East Timor is incorporated into Indonesia.

Online Sources

www.art-pacific.com
A useful site about Oceanic art from many islands of the South Pacific, especially Papua New Guinea. Includes information, pictures, maps, and links to other Web sites.

www.china-fpa.org
Photographs of Igorot tribes from the Philippines showing costumes and tattoos.

www.eastjava.com
Pictures of the architecture and artifacts of the Toraja people of Sulawesi (formerly Celebes), Indonesia.

www.Filipinoheritage.com
A detailed and useful site on Filippino costume, including modern national dress and historical costume.

www.haqq.com.au
A description of the Minangkabau people of West Sumatra, Indonesia.

www.hostkingdom.net
An outline of the countries of Oceania, including information on island names (many of which have changed since independence), ethnic populations, and historical dates.

Further Reading

Barrow, Terence. *Maori Art of New Zealand.* Paris: Unesco Press, 1978.

Kennett, Frances. *World Dress: A Comprehensive Guide to the Folk Costume of the World.* London: Mitchell Beazley, 1994.

Mattet, L. *Arts and Cultures 2002: Antiquity, Africa, Oceania, Asia, Americas 1977–2002.* Paris, France: Vilo Publishers, 2002.

Thomas, Nicholas. *Oceanic Art.* London: Thames and Hudson, 1995.

About the Author

Charlotte Greig is a writer, broadcaster, and journalist. She has written on culture, literature, music, and history. She is author of several books and has contributed newspaper articles to national newspapers *The Guardian* and *The Independent.* Charlotte has an MA in intellectual history from Sussex University.

Index